stay-at-home calls for poetry

By desirae moten

Words To Books LLC

stay-at-home calls for poetry

For information contact :

Website:
https://storiesbydesirae.mailerpage.com/

Email: mail@desiraesstories.com

Cover design by Darrell Moten

Editors: Katie Wismer and Lanette Sweeney

ISBN:

979-8-9852738-4-7 (paperback)

table of contents

"It's hard to be honest."

Desirae Moten

\

"Honesty is often very hard.
The truth is often painful.
But the freedom it can bring
is worth the trying."

Fred Rogers

Chapter One: Built-Up Emotions

<u>all talk</u>

You're all talk and no improvement.

You're all talk and no change.

You're all talk and no movement.

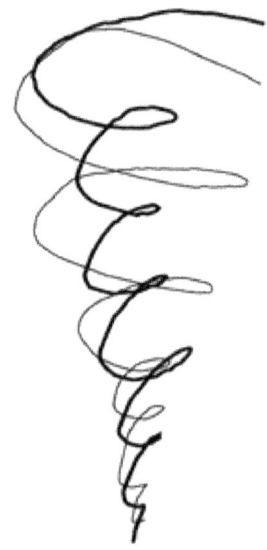

I'm hopeful, then I'm not. Gyrate.

<u>anger turned inward</u>

You ever get so angry
you get hot immediately?

and your chest rises and falls
right in front of your eyes

because the weight is so heavy?
And you lose your appetite?

You just want to lie down
and sink into the space

so the stillness can hold you?
It's defeat.

It's depression.
This battle with life.

All I want to do is call a time-out.

a glimpse of outdoors

Window cracked
just enough

for me to feel the breeze
shared by the summer night.

Dark, but so refreshing.
True nightlife.

I want to wear only a small jacket,
walk with friends,
walk with family,
walk with a loved one.

Swallow this peace
called fresh air.

Instead I'm inside
during stay-at-home time.

This invitation of air pulls me outside,
but my body sits stuck to the chair.

<u>not allowed to be angry</u>

I'm like Bruce Banner,
whose secret is
"I'm always angry."

I'm angry . . .
. . . all the time

My rage is packed down,
stuffed so tight

(inside)

reaching the end of each limb,
each valve,
each cell,
each particle that creates my being.

Quiet.
Don't forget angry.

Giggly.
DON'T forget angry.

Friendly.
DON'T FORGET angry.

Passionate.
DON'T FORGET ANGRY.

6

My secret rage is why
I can have friends
yet feel friendless,

why I can be home with my family
yet feel like I failed my family

why I can write stories
yet not publish more books

why I get annoyed easily, running
thousands of fake scenarios in my head

why I'm so broken
I don't feel like piecing together
my own puzzle

why my head collects
a storm of thoughts I can't set free

why I'm content with being alone,
but wonder . . .

. . . how long I can stay unnoticed
before somebody sees me.

My secret is, I'm always angry,

an angry person
who doesn't get to be angry.

No Hulk gets to surface out of me.

I just want one punch
to feel in control of my life.

Two punches.
Why does progress take so long?

Three punches.
Let me scream to admit how drained I am.

Four, five, six, seven punches.
Please?

How can anger stay suppressed so long?

How can anger be worn and not seen?

You can't hear the hurt because anger
numbs it

My anger is my honesty . . .

. . . waiting to be released.

i'm stressed

I hide so much
I lose count,
lose sleep,
lose words,
lose friends,
but never
lose my temper.

to friendships grown apart: part 1

I'm calling myself out
as an introvert and closed person
who hides parts of me.

My friendships are built on
masks of happiness.

I text, message, or call
only when I'm at a higher
emotional level.

I do this because I never believe friends
can handle or understand the complete me.

I see this isn't fair to myself
nor my friendships.

I see that I choose not to share what is
impacting my life.

I see that I choose not to say
what bothers me.

I see that I thought hanging out was better
than having uncomfortable conversations.

But I need raw,
authentic friendships.

I never felt fully there
because I had personal worries
in the back of my mind.

I never felt fully there
because you, friend,
made talking about your life seem so easy.

Expressing myself
never came that way for me;
so I chose to have conversation
with a filter.

I smile so much,
I've made you think that's who I am.

I'm a mess, and yes, everyone is,
but some people show their mess,
some hide it.

I hide so much it's made me come off as
reserved and uninterested.

My actions put me here,
but I want to be
a more confident person,
a more honest friend.

This poem is my first step.

<u>moving forward</u>

Friendships only work when both sides
feel cared about, included, heard,
acknowledged, and honest.

Simple words
often overlooked,
often neglected,
often unsaid.

I strive to do better.

to friendships grown apart: part 2

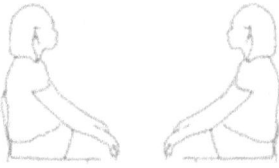

Now I want you, if you consider me a friend
who didn't live up to your expectations,
I want you to call me out.

At least have a conversation
about me, to me.
Message me or ask to video chat.

Then, be honest.

Trust me, you're forever in the back of my
mind because we had good memories.

But if you don't want to tell me what went
wrong or how I hurt you,
then I can't share my side nor apologize.

Yes, there are bigger problems
than lost friendships right now. But friends
keep you sane.
Friends listen.
Friends help.
Friends give you something
to look forward to.

So during this time, friendship shouldn't be an afterthought.

Sorry I took so long to say this.

Your friendship meant a lot to me;
I just didn't know how to keep it alive when you only knew pieces of me.

I am saying I'm sorry to you.

I'm sorry for not texting.
I'm sorry for not hanging out more
and going on trips.
I'm sorry for not being more honest.
I'm sorry for not calling you more.
I'm sorry for not making time for you.
I'm sorry for how we fell off.
I'm sorry.

I really am.

Your friendship carries weight with me
because you had significance in my life.
The shows we bonded over,
the catch-up talks,
the support when making life decisions,
the laughter and inside jokes,
the connection,
the vibe.

You're not forgotten. I hope you don't think of our friendship with regret.

Movies and songs don't depict the pain
of ended friendships enough,
but they mattered.

Friendships don't always end roughly.
Life may just cause us to drift.

Drift apart.
Drift apart for a while.
Drift apart for a second.
Drift apart for some years.
Drift apart for forever.

Please don't forget, though,
technology works both ways.
I'm not the only one who drifted.

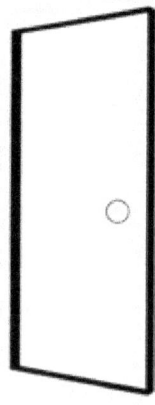

<u>to live and not take a chance</u>

is stagnant living

I self-sabotage.
Will I stop?

Chapter Two: Racing Thoughts

<u>sweets, let's cuddle</u>

a haiku

I miss you. Time moves.

Burdened, but still laughing. Kiss.

Family. Home. Love.

⁛

I miss you.

Family. Home. L –

--ove. Burdened.

why is happiness so hard to keep?

"Are you happy?"

My eyes blink.

My pace slows.

I don't know.

I want to be.

i'm scared

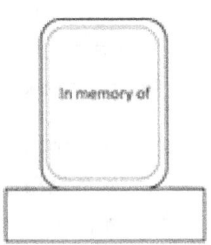

Have you ever thought about the death toll
in our world?

When will it ever be scary enough
to change our behavior?

Do we need to know each person who dies
for death to hurt,

for death to make us question how we're
living?

Before war, weapons, and hate, we all
feared dying from simpler causes:

dying from aging,
dying from lack of medicine,
dying from weather,
dying from injury,
dying in childbirth,
dying from drowning,
dying from hunger.

As medicine advanced,
we learned to fear new
deadly diseases:

dying from cancer,
dying from heart disease,
dying from stroke,
dying from diabetes,
dying from HIV/AIDS.

New machines made us fear:

dying from industrial accidents,
dying in car wrecks,
dying in train derailments,
dying in plane crashes.

Factory farming exposed us to
dying from food poisoning.

On top of that, gun violence
brought fear of:

dying from drive-by shootings,
dying from an accidental shooting,
dying from school shootings,
dying from massacres,
dying from police crimes,
dying from uncontrolled tempers,
dying from road rage,
dying from escalated feuds.

War and bombs make us fear:

dying from an attack,
dying from an invasion,
dying from living on one's native land,
dying from fighting for one's home
or country,

Hate crimes fill us with dread of:

dying for having a certain skin tone,
dying for having a certain belief,
dying for having a voice,
dying for wanting a better education,
dying for seeking a better future,
dying for wanting change,
dying for existing.

Today, death is coming in the form of
safety last, "normal" living first.

Covid-19, climate change,
lack of equity, bring added scares
in a world that's been deteriorating
for too long.

Suicide stems from a battle;
are we going to confront the pain
or double the death rate?

Time is always ticking,
but things feel more closed-in now.
Change needs to happen

because I want to live,
without being scared forever.
So, I'm gonna be scared for just a moment.

I'm gonna be scared for the length
of this poem.

<u>hiding</u>

I'm lying here for you to find,
but I'm hidden under the covers.
You can't see me, and I can't see you.

A galaxy of unspoken reflections
lies between us.

The thoughts keep us awake, separated,
unable to sleep.

Stillness holds us in place.

Silence.

It's surreptitious.

working on being a better friend

I might've chosen a relationship
over our friendship.

I didn't know. Now I realize.
I'm working on being a better friend.

night cries

Overcoming challenges
triggers long night cries.

I struggle through my imposter experience,
with slow tears, snot drips, voice muffled.
I beg to depart from a house boxed in,
where the future is unknown.
Prayerfully.

Say her name.

Acknowledge her life.

Say her name.

Acknowledge her death.

we want to be treated as humans

I am weighed down.
Cops are killing Black people,
acting like that's the job they were given.

White murderers and criminals get arrested,
put politely in police cars.
They get mugshots–
not a video of their last moments.

Innocent white people live their lives,
without being bothered.
Innocent Black people live their lives
being tormented.

She wants to learn.
She wants to grow.
She wants to live.

He wants to learn.
He wants to grow.
He wants to live.

They want to learn.
They want to grow.
They want to live.

Human beings want to learn.
Human beings want to grow.
Human beings want to live.

Even when a crime is committed,
the criminal is human,
wanting to learn,
wanting to grow,
wanting to live.

People understand this
when the criminal is white.

When will Black lives matter?

When will racist people stop seeing
enemies and see what is?

black female reflection

I understand that institutionalized racism
pits the Black community against itself,

that white supremacy divides a community
that they batter,

that the system focuses on black-on-black
crime, that the system doesn't want to
acknowledge the stripping of black rights,
black money, black employment, black
housing, that the system strips equality,
causing Black struggle.

I know the system sees Black people as less
than. That the system surrounds Black
students with teachers who don't always
have their best interests in mind.

At age 13 I see clips of the KKK in class
and I'm sickened by their horrid actions.
Sickened because I can't look at an image
or video of their wrongful hate without
feeling my ancestors to the core. Sickened
because the KKK are real people attacking,
burning, killing, and destroying other
human beings because of their race.
Sickened because I hear my ancestors
telling me not to look only at the pain,
to instead remember their lives.

The system's inequality
hinders black children
going to school.

Public schools are not the issue.

Public schools are neglected, given fewer
resources, supplies, educators. Public
schools are seen as dangerous,
pushing Black parents to send their kids
to private schools.

At 15, I fear my family getting pulled over.
I fear the officers. I fear Pop saying the
wrong thing.

I fear being pressed against our car,
handled and battered. I fear escalation,
weapons in my family's faces. I fear jail
or death.

At age 19, I've heard so many comments
about how I have a white voice. In these
moments, my identity is judged. In these
moments,
I realize there's a lot to explore and unpack
about speech, race, and Blackness.

At 20, I'm watching my brother grow up,
watching him find comfort in hoodies, and
I'm angered that his comfort could make

him look "suspicious." I
watch him wanting to walk around with his
friends; I fear stupid, teenage-boy antics
will result in him getting blamed when he
would be the last to do anything careless
and risky.
I hear Pop tell him to be careful when out
because of his race,
because of him being the only Black
person. I hear him told that white people
could suspect him for being in a suburban
neighborhood, or store, or park, or with his
white friend.

Watching him, I pray for nothing to ever
happen to him. I pray all his dreams can be
reached and not taken from him. I pray he
never has to run for his life. I pray he isn't
traumatized for a crime he didn't do. I pray
for my brother's safety.

I feel agonized to see death after death on
the news. It hurts to see inhumane acts of
racism perpetrated. It hurts to see demands
for justice ignored. It hurts to see minimal
changes to a failed system that exceeds
many lifetimes.

At 21, even at a predominantly white
college, the Black students show me how
beautiful being Black is,

how beautiful Black natural hair is, that I can
wear my hair natural and style it myself,
how beautiful Black confidence is, that I can
embrace that part of myself,
how beautiful Black education is,
connecting with the right professors,
mentors, adults, and peers who will help
me pursue my career goals,
how beautiful Black passion is, self-love and
support for one another.

How beautiful Black voices are, speaking up
about racism, hate, injustice, systemic
oppression, pain, love, memories, family,
art, and one another.

How beautiful Black people are for creating
an environment that builds stamina and
perseverance, showing me, I have to do
more, accept myself, and challenge life.

At 23, I walk down the street eager to shop
at Ross for high-low dresses; I walk happily
until I see cops on bikes. I then walk
conscious of my steps as I come near them.
I walk fearing being stopped. I walk
knowing I did nothing, but worrying they'll
question me anyway.

Yet being in the store doesn't ease my
tension. At the store I am cautious. At the
store I glimpse at cardigans, then glance

back.
At the store I check behind me to see if I'm
being watched.
At the store I am nervous my backpack
makes me look more suspicious.
At the store I fear they'll think I'm stealing
because I'm in one section too long.
At the store when I try on shoes, then take
them off because they don't fit, I fear
people will doubt I actually have the money
to buy the shoes.
At the store, even if no one approaches me,
my thoughts are prepared
for all possible incidents.

When with my group of friends,
the question is asked,
"How do you think you'll die?"
I answer, "I think I'll be shot."

<u>pied beauty</u>
<u>after Gerard Manley Hopkins</u>

It feels like People of Color can't win.

A breakthrough happens, then shatters.

Our hearts are just so heavy.

Our want for change is undeniably worth it.

Our meraki will continue to flourish.

But life is full of hurt.

Just let us have a chance.

No. Give us our living right

To be in this world unafraid.

Let "Pied Beauty" run the world.

My goal is to contribute change.

introducing the D and Des show!

Tonight's all laughter.
Only childhood jokes
that no one else was there for but us.
Nicknames only we know.
Stories we've told a hundred times
and we'll tell a hundred more times
to each other.

Did I mention it's a three-hour show?

Full of sharing new ideas.
Stories we're working on,
plots we want to finish,
shows and movies that keep us passionate.
The content that keeps us invested,
inspired, connected, that we'd spend hours
sharing with each other, and no one else.

Time check!

Now for the role-play portion.
Creating scenarios of our future wins.
How will our premieres look?
What about our acceptance speeches?
What celebrities will we meet?
What project will we work on next
and with whom? Are we celebrities now?
What will our fame pictures look like?

Where will we live and how often will we
visit each other?

Time check!

I enjoy doing this with you,
my brother.
Getting off topic when we never had an
agenda to begin with.
We reminisce, create, think, joke, annoy,
listen, and bond on this show
that you and I created
when we were just kids.
Side by side in a chair
with a laptop
and a low-quality camera,
being random.
Being siblings.

We'll do it again, but for now,
we're the hosts and the audience,
and we're applauding each other
before we depart and get to work.

Until next time,
on the D and Des show.

<u>i want to give you peace</u>
<u>(complacency needs to go. a goodbye.)</u>

You shouldn't know the pain of working mornings and nights.

You shouldn't know the pain of having dreams that are still hard to make a reality.

You shouldn't know the pain of being so tired your body is functioning against your energy.

Life should not have told you there's no time to relax.

Life should not have told you to give and purchase more than save.

Life should not have told you you will enjoy things when . . .

Life should not have told you to wait, to enjoy things someday . . .

You should be able to enjoy things now!

Money issues, we pray for help.
Money issues, we pray for money.
Money issues, we pray for fulfillment.

I'm sorry I have not made enough (yet)
to buy you the house you've always
wanted.

I'm sorry I have not made enough (yet)
so you don't have to worry and stress.

I'm sorry I have not made enough (yet)
so you don't have to be exhausted.

I will let complacency go so we can step
into our future.

I will let hesitation go so we can step into
our future.

I will let waiting go, so we can step into our
future.

No more homemade excuses. I want to
release the tension from your bodies.

I want to see the dreams we've been
working for.

I want you to see the dreams you've been
working towards.

Mom, Pop, I want you to be at ease,
comfortable, and excited.

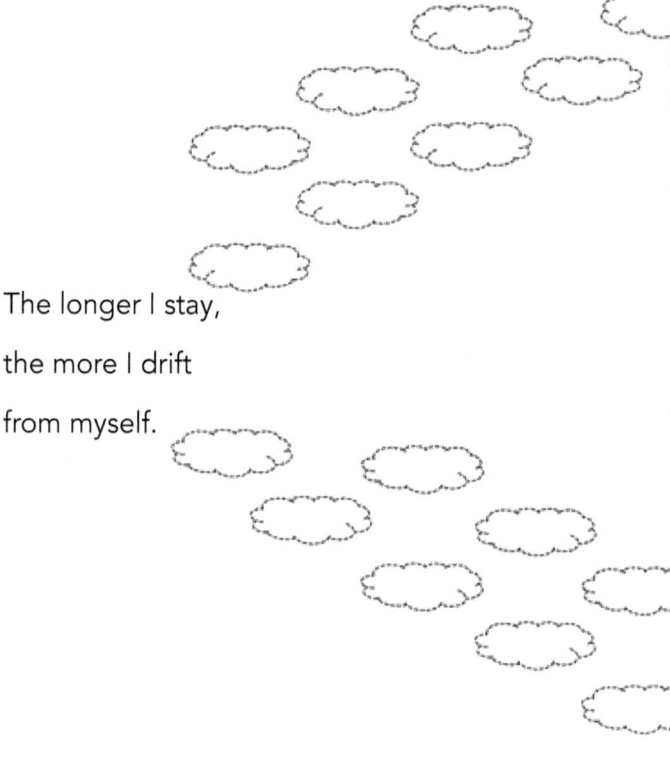

The longer I stay,

the more I drift

from myself.

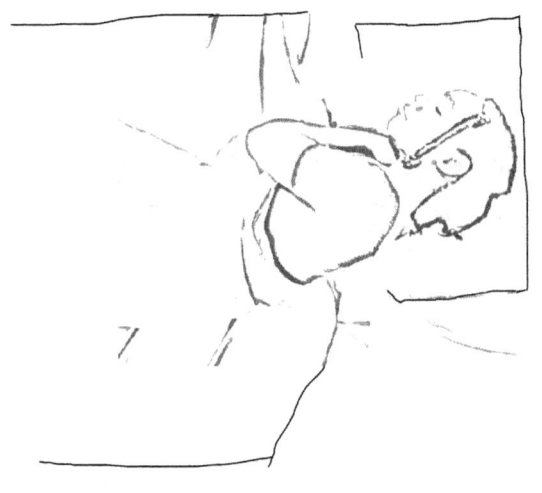

Chapter Three: Where Do I Go From Here?[1]

---

[1] Song: Where Do I Go From Here by Sebastian Mego

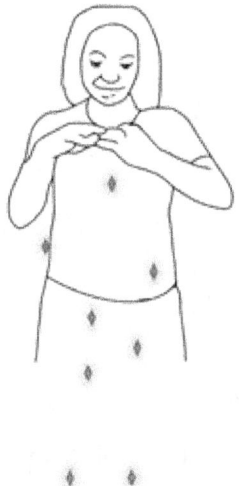

You help Earth. Earth helps you.

Desirae, why?

Why do you feed yourself negative words?

Why is it hard for you to believe in yourself?

Why do you forget the good in every day?

Why do you feel stuck?

Why do you let yourself procrastinate?

Why are you waiting?

Why do you want to give up when you made it this far?

Why do you hold all your emotions in?

Why are you scared?

Why don't you digest the motivational words you hear every day?

Why do you forget you have greatness in you?

Why is it hard for you to ask for help?

Why hide your voice?

Why hide who you are?

doubt doubt

I believe others doubt me.

So I start to doubt myself.

I don't like doing that.

I know I will accomplish and achieve

what is meant for me.

My manifest.

Inhale. Exhale. Release.

Allowing my heart to stop feeling heavy.

Talk it out. Don't be afraid.

I started with anger and am finding
movement towards building happiness.

Fluctuating,

but growing.

i'm ready

I'm ready for the world

to see itself

below the surface

down deeper–

for humankind to see

how we have steered off the path of being
humane.

"It takes time to learn yourself." – Dempsy[2]

I've been repeatedly hearing this lately:
It takes time,
a daily process,
an ongoing learning.

Deep breaths,
subconscious talks,
constant reminders to stop:
stop negative thinking,
stop procrastinating,
stop getting upset
stop making up scenarios
that probably won't happen,
stop wasting time,
stop delaying my plans.

Open my eyes to the present,
do something with this time I have.

Learn myself.

I'm still learning me.
I will make mistakes.
I still have new stages to enter,
experiences that haven't happened yet.

I don't want to let me down

---

[2] https://linktr.ee/dempsy

I don't want to die not having embraced all
my potential

I want to push myself forward

Like an arrow
I've been pulled back for too long
I'm ready to soar, scared
to take my own breath away.
I want to gain peace
to remember gratitude
and happiness in every day.

I want to take the time to learn myself
because there's only one me
and I deserve to live seen

It'll take time
but I'm worth it.

I'm going to take it one inhale
and exhale at a time.

My eyes close.
My eyes open.

I enter the stage of loving me.

<u>to Desirae</u>

Don't sell yourself short.

Don't hold yourself back.

Don't contemplate the what ifs.

Don't wait any longer.

Don't use your struggle as an excuse.

Don't hide who you are . . .

Use the beautiful parts of you
that make up all of you.

Accept what God is showing you.
Accept who you are.

Let yourself desire your goals
and achieve them.

There is only one you
and you matter in this world.

Don't forget that.

<u>unapologetic</u>

I'm a Black person,

with a voice,

in a body,

trying to learn

how to be

unapologetically

me.

Desirae's 2020 and 2021 steps to
becoming unapologetically me:
mind, body, soul

1. Listen to God to understand the choices I'm supposed to make compared to the ones I'm choosing to make.

2. Learn to say, "I was wrong" or "You were right." I need to think before I speak, so I am able to say, "You are right," instead of needing to be right myself.

3. Act on the motto, "Say what you want, but I know the truth." You can say and think what you want about me or my choices, but God and I know the truth, so I need to go forward with that truth in mind.

4. Be in tune with my body. Listening to my body's needs and growing and working with it is so refreshing. I'm not using my body; I am knowing my body and becoming more acquainted, connected, and patient.

5. Know when I really do need a day to do nothing but chill and take a breather.

6. Never be ashamed that my family comes first.

7. Stop self-sabotaging my opportunities, especially writing opportunities with friends. I'm sorry I said no to the people who invited me to write with them. I was too shy or doubted myself too much to accept past offers, even though the support would've been beneficial. I'm used to being by myself, so I thought it always had to be that way. But it doesn't. I realize I missed out on some growth. I'm glad I can do better for myself in the future.

8. Thank God everyday (by writing or praying).

9. Listen when I hear God's voice telling me "No" as I start to make negative choices. That's when I know I am doing something I need to stop. So I repeat to myself, "No." Then I do something productive and beneficial for myself.

10. Have friends with whom I talk monthly, if not weekly with. This is something I finally understand I want so that I know we both care and are checking in on each other. This does not mean the people I talk to less frequently are not friends, but for me they're not close friends unless we've talked

and made a mutual agreement of our infrequent communication.

11. Start therapy. On June 15th, 2021, I met a woman who offered embodiment resources for Black women, one of the first new people I talked to since the pandemic began. Talking to her gave me the urge to overshare, but I knew she wasn't a therapist, so I refrained. This made me realize I was ready for therapy and ready to stop telling myself, "I don't want to go to therapy because it's too much to share and I wish the therapist had followed me throughout my life and already knew what I was going through. It's too late to go now." I see, now, that I DO want to share my story with someone. I know it'll be hard, and it might not even be this summer that I go, but I know I will go and that's progress.

12. Be ready to apologize—and think before I speak so I give myself fewer reasons to be sorry. I am aware now of when I am in the wrong or spoke too fast without thinking. I talk to God about it immediately after and apologize. But I need to work on, in the moment, being kinder and preparing what I want to say to the people I am talking to. I need to use a gentler tone of voice with my family, boyfriend, friends, or strangers,

instead of commenting immediately in a voice that sounds annoyed or ungrateful or like I'm complaining.

13. Believe in my growth. I have changed. It may not seem like much to others, but regardless of the slow progress, I'm doing a lot better than in previous years and that deserves to be acknowledged.

14. Embrace my love of Black women's breathwork sessions. I joined Black Girls Breathing (bgb), and it has made me learn so much more about my feelings and actions. Plus, being surrounded by other Black women makes me feel more connected and heard. It allows a bond that I've been needing. I am not alone. Plus, the support and honesty from Black women is empowering. This space is helping me grow.

15. Deep breaths! I have to mention breathwork a second time, this time focusing on being in tune with my body. Deep breaths have centered me so much and brought a new relaxation to my life. Inhale. Exhale. I'm listening to my body's needs and pains and wants.

16. Forgive myself and others. I have entered the forgiveness stage. It will be a

long journey. I will be exploring what I've been holding on to. There is a lot to understand, but entering this stage is eye opening.

There are more steps I have not reached yet. I still need to handle the racing thoughts and scenarios that constantly play in my head. I do not know how to release that stress to be able to breathe a little easier as me. Nor, have I figured out yet how to eliminate negative thoughts.

But I know God will walk me through each step. I know I will learn and grow and change and transform. I am ready for this process and encouraging it to happen. I am determined and willing to own my flaws.

Thanks for reading! Please leave a short review of what you thought!

Connect with me on social media:

Instagram: @storiesbydesirae

Website: storiesbydesirae.mailerpage.com

YouTube: storiesbydesirae

About the Author

Desirae Moten lives on the East Coast of the United States. She enjoys working with kids and helping people. Her first form of writing was poetry and from there grew to short stories, novellas, novels, and recently children's books. When she's not writing, you can catch her adding movies and TV shows to her growing list of things she needs to watch–or going down a YouTube hole. Her favorite food is pizza (cheese, or green peppers only on the right side, or margherita). She finds it fitting that her first published book is a poetry collection because poetry was the first form of creative writing for which she took classes outside of school, starting when she was in third grade.

If you'd like to know what Desirae is working on next, you can sign up for her newsletter: storiesbydesirae.mailerpage.com

Acknowledgments

Thank you for taking the time to read my journey of discovering myself and becoming unapologetically me. It has taken me some time to get here. I hope my poetry connected with you, spoke to you, or comforted you in some way.

I want to thank everyone who has impacted and been a part of my life to shape who I am today. I want to thank all who have supported me (my family, teachers, professors, friends, loved ones, peers, and you, reader) and encouraged my passion for writing throughout the years.

I want to end with thanking God for guiding and blessing me.